D-DAY!

THE CANADIANS AND THE NORMANDY LANDINGS JUNE 1944

by

Dr. Reg H. Roy

Access to History No. 6

CEF BOOKS
2001

Canadian Cataloguing in Publication Data
Roy, Reginald H., (1922-
D-Day! : the Canadians and the Normandy landings, 1944
(Access to history series; no. 6)
Includes bibliographical references.
ISBN 1-896979-38-6
1. World War, 1939-1945—Campaigns—France—Normandy. 2. Canada. Canadian Army—History—World War, 1939-1945. I. Title. II. Series: Access to History series; no. 6.

D756.5.N6R692 2001 940.54'2142 C00-901677-7

Published by:
CEF BOOKS
PO BOX 40083,
OTTAWA, ONTARIO K1V 0W8
613-823-7000

This book is dedicated to the memory of the 110,000 Canadians who willingly gave their lives in the defence of freedom in the Twentieth Century.

Lest We Forget

Acknowledgements:
We would like to thank Ontario Command of The Royal Canadian Legion and the Department of Canadian Heritage for the support which made this series possible. Additional thanks to Mr. Brian McClean and Mr. Dan Charbonneau for their valuable contributions to this book.

Publication of this book has been supported by the Canadian War Museum.

Front cover: D-Day-The Assault by O.N. Fisher (CWM 12469)

"There have been only a handful of days since the beginning of time on which the direction the world was taking has been changed for the better in one twenty-four hour period by an act of man. June 6, 1944, was one of them.

What the Americans, British and Canadians were trying to do was get back a whole continent that had been taken from its rightful owners and whose citizens had been taken captive by Adolf Hitler's German army. It was one of the most monumentally unselfish things one group of people ever did for another."

Andy A. Rooney, Private, United States Army.

SUPREME HEADQUARTERS
ALLIED EXPEDITIONARY FORCE

Soldiers, Sailors and Airmen of the Allied Expeditionary Force!

You are about to embark upon the Great Crusade, toward which we have striven these many months. The eyes of the world are upon you. The hopes and prayers of liberty-loving people everywhere march with you. In company with our brave Allies and brothers-in-arms on other Fronts, you will bring about the destruction of the German war machine, the elimination of Nazi tyranny over the oppressed peoples of Europe, and security for ourselves in a free world.

Your task will not be an easy one. Your enemy is well trained, well equipped and battle-hardened. He will fight savagely.

But this is the year 1944! Much has happened since the Nazi triumphs of 1940-41. The United Nations have inflicted upon the Germans great defeats, in open battle, man-to-man. Our air offensive has seriously reduced their strength in the air and their capacity to wage war on the ground. Our Home Fronts have given us an overwhelming superiority in weapons and munitions of war, and placed at our disposal great reserves of trained fighting men. The tide has turned! The free men of the world are marching together to Victory!

I have full confidence in your courage, devotion to duty and skill in battle. We will accept nothing less than full Victory!

Good Luck! And let us all beseech the blessing of Almighty God upon this great and noble undertaking.

Dwight D. Eisenhower

Table of Contents

FORTRESS EUROPE - JUNE 1943

Introduction

For the Western Allies, the invasion of France on June 6th, 1944 was one of the most critical battles of the war. Four years earlier, the German Army swept over the borders of Holland, Belgium and France inflicting a crushing defeat on all who stood in its way. In May 1940, at Dunkirk, most of the British Army in France had been evacuated but with the loss of massive amounts of equipment.

In the months that followed, the Germans were to conquer or dominate the rest of Europe and launch a furious aerial attack on Great Britain as a prelude to invasion. In the Autumn of 1940, as German fighter and bomber aircraft fought in the skies over Britain, they were met and defeated by the Royal Air Force. The German invasion was called off and Adolph Hitler, the Nazi dictator of Germany, decided to launch his armies against Russia in June, 1941.

By this time Italy had allied itself with Germany. Six months later, on the other side of the world, Japan attacked the American naval base at Pearl Harbour. Japanese forces swept around South East Asia to the border of India, occupying British, Dutch, French and Portuguese colonies one after another.

The year 1942 was a dark one for the Allies. Germany had penetrated deeply into Russia and dominated the Balkans. In North Africa, the German-Italian armies had entered Egypt to reach El Alamein. In the Pacific, Japanese forces occupied most of Burma, the Dutch East Indies, Malaya, French Indo-China and the Philippines. On all fronts the Allied defences were stretched to the breaking point while at sea, German U-boats were coming close to cutting the essential flow of supplies from North America to Great Britain.

It was only by a mighty effort that the Allies managed to stop the surge of German and Japanese victories and, with gathering strength, began to turn the tide of battle. In the Pacific, American and Allied naval ships halted Japan's expansion and went on the offensive. In North Africa, British Empire forces, and later the Americans, overcame the German and Italian armies and, by the summer of 1943, had invaded Sicily and Italy.

Since 1941 the brunt of the German attacks had been borne by the Russians. Millions of men had been locked in battle on the Eastern Front.

Casualties were very high and Russia had been pleading with the Allies to establish a Second Front in France to help relieve the pressure on them.

To cross the English Channel with a force sufficient to guarantee a successful assault took time. First, the Allies had to ensure that they dominated the skies over Europe. Second, the "Battle of the Atlantic" had to be won and the U-boat menace reduced to manageable levels. Third, five seaborne and three airborne divisions had to receive special training for the assault on the French coast, all supported by thousands of naval vessels and aircraft. In Great Britain an immense collection of tanks, ammunition, artillery, vehicles, food supplies and other warlike stores had to be assembled for shipment to the invading armies as well as further divisions to reinforce those landed.

By 1944, all of the above conditions had been met. When and where the landings would take place were highly guarded secrets. An assault from the sea, however, was a critical gamble and leaders of the British, Canadian and American troops knew it. No matter how carefully plans had been made, poor weather could destroy months of preparation or the loss of secrecy could alert the German defenders. Opening the Second Front would be a turning point in the history of the Second World War. Canadian troops were to be in the forefront of the battle.

View from a Canadian Landing Craft enroute to France, June 5, 1944.

(PAC PA 137014)

Historical Overview

By the summer of 1944 the Second World War had been raging for almost five years. Hitler's armies had invaded Poland in September, 1939. France and Great Britain mobilized their forces to fight Germany but early in 1940 the Germans launched an attack which defeated the French and sent the British Army back over the English Channel. The Germans over-ran Norway, the Netherlands, Belgium, Czechoslovakia and other European countries in rapid succession. By late 1940 Italy, now allied to Germany, carried the War to North Africa. In June, 1941 Hitler widened the War when German forces attacked Russia. About six months later the War became truly global when Japan attacked the United States at Pearl Harbour.

At first the Axis powers - Germany, Japan and Italy - achieved tremendous successes. As the Allies gained strength and built up their War production, the tide changed. Slowly but surely huge Russian armies pushed the Germans westward. In North Africa, British and later American forces defeated the German and Italian armies and in 1943 Sicily and Italy were invaded. In the air, Allied aircraft hammered Germany with growing intensity while at sea the unrelenting attacks against the U-boats lessened the threat to convoys bringing arms and men to Great Britain.

Canada to 1944

Canada had declared War on Germany on September 10th, 1939. It was terribly unprepared for any military conflict but nevertheless it sent over 16,000 men of the 1st Canadian Infantry Division to Britain in December, 1939. Within a few years the Canadian contribution to the War effort increased at a remarkable rate as the navy, army and air force grew at an unprecedented scale. By June, 1943 the army alone had three infantry divisions, two armoured divisions and two armoured brigades in the United Kingdom. A month later the 1st Canadian Infantry Division and 2nd Canadian Armoured Brigade were fighting in Sicily. They were joined later by the 5th Canadian Armoured Division to form II Canadian Corps. By the end of 1943 more than 240,000 Canadian soldiers were in Europe.

While Canadian forces were fighting in Italy, the remaining Canadian formations were undergoing intensive training in Great Britain.

For years the Allies realized that if they were to deliver a knock-out blow to the German army they must launch a cross-Channel invasion of France. This could be done only when they achieved air and naval superiority. In addition they had to build a great variety of large and small craft capable of landing thousands of men and hundreds of tanks on the beaches. The initial assault, codenamed Operation "Neptune", would be a combined operation involving the navy, army and air force. It would be part of the larger operation, codenamed "Overlord", which involved also the fighting inland from the beaches, the build-up of forces and the break-out into central France.

By the late Spring of 1944 there was no concealing the massive preparations being made in Britain to launch an attack on German-occupied France. Throughout Southern England there were huge tented camps containing Allied assault troops. There were fields covered with tanks and ammunition depots, trucks and armoured vehicles, gliders for airborne paratroopers and huge dumps of military supplies, hospital stores and engineering equipment. Someone said at the time that only the barrage-balloons were preventing Southern England from sinking under the weight of the massive amounts of munitions and equipment.

The German Defences - The Atlantic Wall

The Germans knew that, sooner or later, they could expect an attack from the sea. Slowly at first, but then with quickening speed and energy, they began to fortify the coast of France. Huge coastal guns in thick reinforced concrete emplacements menaced potential landing sites. These were most numerous in the areas of ports and harbours which the Germans felt the Allies must seize to bring in thousands of tons of supplies to maintain their forces on shore. Open beaches were covered with wooden stakes and iron obstacles designed to rip out or blow up the hulls of landing craft. Covering the beaches were field guns and machine-gun posts placed to mow down invaders as they stormed out of their craft. Mortar and infantry positions, protected by barbed wire, were scattered all along the coast and seaside houses were reinforced with sandbags to give the defenders more protection. Further inland there were minefields, roadblocks, infantry bunkers, and flooded areas. Many open fields were studded with poles to destroy Allied gliders, while at key positions heavy guns were sited to bring down a crushing weight of steel on the invaders.

The Atlantic Wall by O.N. Fisher

(CWM 12416)

"We must stop the enemy in the water and destroy his equipment while it is still afloat... We must, in the short time left, bring all the defences up to such a standard that they will be proof against the strongest attack."
Erwin Rommel, Commander of the German's coastal defences

"This was the Atlantic Wall. It was not one solid line of gigantic concrete forts... It was a series of formidable casements, the largest about 30 or 40 feet square, with walls 4 or 5 feet thick - all reinforced concrete. Between these casements were lines of concrete pillboxes, dug deep into the ground with just the top above the earth. Trench systems and tunnels also linked each strong point and there was not a yard of the beach that the cross-fire from machine-guns and rifles could not cover. There were 3 or 4 lines of pillboxes at more vulnerable spots and for 500 or 600 yards inland this belt of bristling positions extended from the shore."
Ross Munro, Canadian War Correspondent.

These fortifications stretched along the coasts of the Netherlands, Belgium and France. In this area, both along the coast and behind it, there were sixty German divisions, totalling 850,000 soldiers, of which ten were panzer (armoured) or panzer grenadier. In overall command was Field Marshal Gerd von Rundstedt. Field Marshal Erwin Rommel, who had fought the Allies in North Africa, was given command of the German forces located in the area where it was felt the Allies would most likely assault. These two men had different opinions respecting the best means of defeating an Allied invasion. Rommel had experienced the devastating blows which Allied bombers could deliver to German tanks and vehicles moving along roads and railways. He felt the German armoured divisions should be positioned close to the coast and be used to defeat the invaders on the beaches. Von Rundstedt, on the other hand, felt the Allies would breach the coastal fortifications. When the main thrust of the invasion was located, then was the time to concentrate the panzer divisions and hurl them against the invaders. Hitler listened to both arguments and decided on a partial compromise which included his decision that the panzer divisions would be released for combat only on his orders.

The problem facing both field marshals was that although they knew the invasion would be launched in 1944, they did not know when or where. German reconnaissance aircraft speeding across the Channel could photograph the growing number of landing craft in English harbours and the build-up of massive supplies in the coastal region. It was felt that the most likely invasion area would be in the Pas de Calais. It was the shortest distance from England, only 60 km, which, in turn would allow a rapid turn-around time for ships carrying troops and supplies. It was close to Calais and other nearby ports which could provide the Allies with harbours to build up the stream of men and supplies needed to maintain the invasion. For these reasons the Germans made this the most heavily defended area along the entire French coast.

Opposing Armies

At the time the Allies invaded France, there were sixty German divisions in France and Belgium. These were divided among four armies. The Fifteenth Army, responsible for the area stretching from the Dutch border to Caen, was the strongest as it was closest to England. The Seventh Army, adjoining it, guarded Normandy and Brittany. South of the Loire were the First Army stretched along the Bay of Biscay and the Nineteenth Army guarding the Mediterranean coast.

In overall charge of these armies was Field-Marshal Gerd von Rundstedt who, earlier, had led German Armies attacking Poland and France. Field-Marshal Erwin Rommel, who commanded a panzer (armoured) division at the outset of the war and later made his reputation leading the Afrika Corps, was given operational command of the two strongest armies, the Fifteenth and Seventh. He would direct the German battle when the invasion began.

Unlike the Allies, the Germans had no single supreme commander in France who had operational authority over the navy, army and air force. Hitler reserved that right for himself. Four of the best German panzer divisions in France, for example, could not be sent into action without the express approval of Hitler. His interference with the plans of his generals would have disastrous consequences for the German forces.

The Supreme Commander of the Allied Expeditionary Force in Western Europe was an American, General Dwight D. Eisenhower, whose previous experience was in the Mediterranean. Serving under him was a British officer, General Bernard Montgomery, who had met and defeated Rommel in North Africa. Montgomery would have operational control of the British Second Army (Lt-Gen. M.C. Dempsey) and the American First

Army (Lt-Gen. Omar N. Bradley), the two attacking formations during the initial phase of the invasion until more divisions could be landed in France to create more armies. The Canadian forces, for example, would go into action as part of the British Second Army. As more Canadian divisions were landed, they would be grouped into the First Canadian Army under the command of a Canadian, Lieutenant-General Harry Crerar.

General Eisenhower, fortunately, was not bothered by any overlapping of command or direct interference from senior politicians as was the case with Von Rundstedt and Rommel. The commander of the Allied naval forces - British, American, Canadian and others - involved in the invasion was a British admiral, Sir Bertram Ramsay. Air Chief Marshal Sir T.L. Leigh Mallory, another British officer with wide experience, commanded the Allied Expeditionary Air Force. As Supreme Commander, Eisenhower could control and direct the efforts of both the naval and air forces to ensure the invasion was successful.

To command such a variety of forces composed of men from a number of different nations demanded a great deal of skill and diplomacy. Eisenhower was ideal for the post, even though a number of his subordinates had more experience in battle than he had. In the end Eisenhower would command a force of 3 million men of which 1.7 million were Americans.

The Allied Plan; Strategic Considerations for the Invasion

It was partly because of the strength of the Atlantic Wall in the Pas de Calais that Allied staff officers, working on an invasion plan during 1943, decided to use the coast of Normandy for the assault. It was further away from England but well within fighter aircraft range. It had a number of wide beaches suitable for landing craft. Just beyond the coast were areas where temporary airfields could be constructed and the large port of Cherbourg lay at the tip of the Normandy peninsula. This area was not as well defended as the Pas de Calais nor were there as many enemy divisions behind the coast. To make up for the lack of good harbours in the initial phases of the assault, the Allies began to work on two large artificial harbours made up of floating piers, caissons and block ships. These could be used to unload the thousands of tonnes of supplies needed to maintain the Allied divisions per day.

The Beaches, Weather Conditions and Tides

Planning for the invasion was an immense affair involving all three services; Army, Navy and Air Force. Weather and timing were particularly important. Some 5,000 ships would be involved in taking five divisions of infantry and 12,000 vehicles across 140 km of the English Channel. A storm could scatter this tremendous armada which could defeat the entire purpose of the operation. Similar concerns affected the air force. Heavy and light bombers were to pound the coastal fortifications before the troops landed. Hundreds of other aircraft were to carry paratroopers and tow gliders full of airborne troops to seize vital enemy targets. These aircraft required fairly clear skies and light winds to meet with success.

The tides had to be considered also. At low tide all the beach obstacles would be exposed and either be avoided or destroyed by engineers. However this meant the landing craft would discharge the assaulting troops hundreds of yards from dry land. There was no protection from enemy fire as the men raced across the open beaches. They would be the killing grounds Rommel envisioned. To land at high tide meant the risk of the craft being sunk by submerged beach obstacles. It was decided, therefore, to land at mid-tide when the upper portions of the obstacles could be seen while at the same time the troops, protected by the steel sides of their craft, could be landed closer to their objective.

The beaches had to be checked beforehand by specially trained naval personnel to ensure they were suitable for the traffic of tanks and vehicles which would be landed on D-Day, the codename for the actual day of the invasion. This was one of the lessons learned from the disastrous attack on Dieppe two years earlier. It was also realized that to overcome and neutralize the beach defences special equipment would be needed. One result of this was the creation of the D-D (Duplex Drive) tanks. This was a 30 tonne, Sherman tank equipped with twin propellers and a water-tight canvas flotation collar attached to its hull above the tracks. With the canvas sides extended above the turret, the tanks could be launched from an LST (landing ships, tank) and "swim" to the beach. These D-D Tanks were to play a vital role on D-Day, especially on the British and Canadian beaches. There were other special tanks as well. One was a tank equipped with a flail of large chains designed to beat the ground in front of it and so detonate mines in its path. Another was a Churchill tank equipped with a heavy mortar to destroy enemy concrete gun emplacements and fortifications.

Secrecy and Deception; Operation "Fortitude"

It was extremely important, naturally, that the enemy should not know when or where the Allies would land. Plans for Operation "Overlord" were given a special category of secrecy and even the officers in the regiments landing on the beaches did not know when the invasion would be until the last moment. Aircraft attacking French railway, bridges, canal locks and roads scattered their raids up and down the coast so as not to indicate Normandy as a special area to be isolated. As D-Day drew near, restrictions on travel to the southern coast of England were imposed on the civilian population and censorship became more stringent.

Hand in hand with the effort to draw a veil of secrecy over Allied invasion plans there was a major attempt to deceive the Germans as to where and in what strength the blows would fall. A number of enemy agents in Britain had been captured and persuaded to act for the Allies by sending fake information to their German masters. One result of this, for example, was that the Germans thought that in May, 1944 there were some eighty Allied divisions in Britain. They also believed there were enough landing craft and ships to carry sixteen divisions across the channel. This was double the number of divisions actually available and triple the amount of shipping the Allies could muster. Working on these false intelligence reports made the Germans feel the Allies might launch two invasions, a small one as a feint to draw German divisions toward it and then the main invasion on a coastal sector which had its counter-attack formations taken from it by the feint. This was to be very useful to Allied strategists.

Operation "Fortitude", the Allied codename for the overall deception scheme, was also designed to make the enemy believe that the main assault would strike the Pas de Calais area. Large camps were erected in England along the coast where the enemy expected the Allies would concentrate. Dummy tanks, artillery, gliders and trucks were erected in fields to simulate real equipment and false radio traffic was established to maintain the enemy's belief that a second invasion force was gathered in the area. These camps and concentrations, however, contained very few troops - only enough to indicate some movement and so reinforce the Germans belief that the initial invasion was a feint. Operation "Fortitude" was a battle of deception that was overwhelmingly successful before, during and after the assault on the beaches began.

The Allied Plan; Infantry and Air Assault

"It is now clear that (Rommel's) intention is to defeat us on the beaches... We must blast our way ashore and get a good lodgement before he can bring up sufficient reserves to turn us out... The land battle will be a terrific party and we shall require the support of the air (forces) all the time - and laid quickly."
Bernard Montgomery, Commanding the Allied invasion forces.

Planning for the invasion of France began to take shape in the summer of 1943. After a careful examination of potential landing areas, and taking into consideration the requirements of the naval, army and air force, it was decided that Normandy would be the target. Five infantry divisions, supported by armour, would land from the sea along an 80 km front. Preceding them would be the British 6th Airborne Division and the 82nd and 101st U.S. Airborne Divisions. These forces would strike at a series of beaches stretching roughly from Cabourg in the east to Varaville in the west. The front was divided into two parts with the First United States Army landing on "Utah" and "Omaha" Beaches and the Second British Army (including the Canadians) landing on "Gold", "Juno", and "Sword" Beaches. On either flank paratroopers and airborne troops were to land hours before the assault from the sea in order to seize vital bridges, crossroads and other objectives to help the invading forces move inland and to blunt the expected German counter attack.

A massive bombardment of the beach defences was planned to help the infantry get through the defence network the enemy had been building for years. One thousand Allied bombers were to strike at these fortifications before the landings took place. This would be followed by naval gunfire from more than 200 major warships. Even as the landing craft approached the beaches special boats equipped to fire artillery and rockets would be coming in to pound enemy defences up to the last minute.

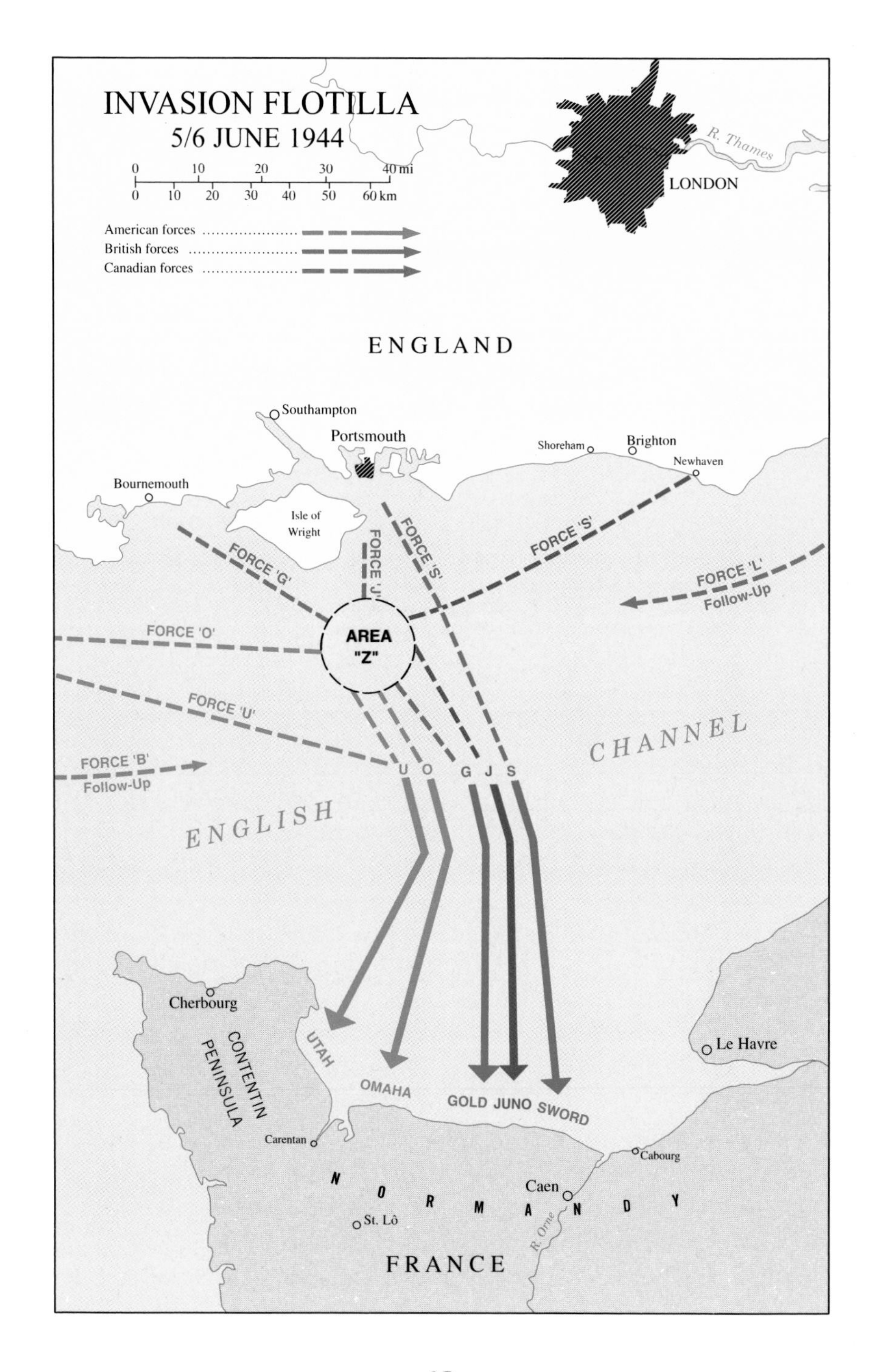
INVASION FLOTILLA
5/6 JUNE 1944
0 10 20 30 40 mi
0 10 20 30 40 50 60 km
American forces
British forces
Canadian forces
LONDON
R. Thames
ENGLAND
Southampton
Portsmouth
Shoreham
Brighton
Newhaven
Bournemouth
Isle of Wright
FORCE 'G'
FORCE 'J'
FORCE 'S'
FORCE 'S'
FORCE 'L' Follow-Up
FORCE 'O'
AREA "Z"
FORCE 'U'
FORCE 'B' Follow-Up
U O G J S
ENGLISH CHANNEL
Cherbourg
CONTENTIN PENINSULA
UTAH
OMAHA
GOLD JUNO SWORD
Le Havre
Carentan
Cabourg
Caen
NORMANDY
St. Lô
R. Orne
FRANCE

The Landings

The initial task of each assault division was to capture and secure a beachhead and thrust inland as far as possible. This would provide room for the thousands of men and vehicles coming in as reinforcements. It would also provide enough room to cushion the expected armoured counter-attack. The next step would be to connect the beaches and push inland to form a lodgement area large enough to accommodate the follow-up divisions. When these had landed in sufficient number, then the plan called for a break out which, it was hoped, would result in the capture of all of Normandy and Brittany. With additional divisions coming in each week, the allied front would then swing up to the Seine River, thus setting the stage for the defeat of all German troops in France.

With plans completed and thousands of men, ships and aircraft gathered along the southern coast of England, the last step to be taken was to decide the time when this formidable power would attack. After examining weather records it was found that the best probable time for meeting the requirements of tide, moonlight and fairly calm seas was during the last week in May and the first week in June. When the decision was made to land at half tide shortly after dawn, the number of suitable days was limited even further. The Supreme Commander of the Allied Expeditionary Force, General Dwight D. Eisenhower, selected June 5th for D-Day, the day the invasion would be launched. Several days before that date the weather began to deteriorate but on the 4th the meteorologist predicted a break in the weather on the 6th. Eisenhower, after consulting with his senior commanders, decided June 6th would be the day. Across the English Channel when strong winds, rain and crashing waves made a landing unlikely for some time, Field-Marshal Rommel had gone to Germany to be with his wife on her birthday.

"I am quite positive we must give the order. I don't like it, but there it is. I don't see how we can do anything else... Okay, we'll go."
Dwight Eisenhower, Supreme Commander of all Allied forces, giving the order to launch "Overlord", in less than optimum weather conditions

---

Probably the most astonishing thing about the invasion was the fact that the greatest armada of ships ever to leave Great Britain sailed 140 km across the English Channel towards German-occupied France without being detected. It was a masterpiece of secrecy, planning, deception and, one must admit, good luck. Operation "Fortitude", the deception scheme, was an amazing success and it was to continue to confuse the enemy for another five or six weeks.

D-Day, Tuesday, June 6th, 1944

Wind - Westnorthwest - force 4.
Sea - Moderate - waves 3-4 feet
Sky - Fair to cloudy with cloud increasing
The weather for June 6th, 1944.

"You will enter the continent of Europe and, in conjunction with the other Allied Nations, undertake operations aimed at the heart of Germany and the destruction of her armed forces.."
Directive to Dwight Eisenhower, Supreme Commander, Allied forces.

The Armada Sails

On the evening of June 5th the great movement of ships began. They were well out to sea when 18,000 paratroopers climbed into aircraft and gliders. As they flew over the Channel before midnight they could see ships of every size and description headed towards the French coast. Mine-sweepers had been at work, well before dusk clearing paths through the minefields laid by the German navy. For the paratroopers, and particularly those coming in by gliders, they would land in the middle of the German fortifications hoping they would avoid land mines and the stakes planted in the open fields along the coast. Their great asset was surprise. Their objective, both on the east and west of the seventy kilometre invasion area, was to seize certain bridges, causeways over flooded areas, gun emplacements and cross roads which would help the invaders move inland and at the same time, prevent German counter-attacks on the invasion beaches. Even as they were preparing to take off, code messages were being broadcast to French Resistance groups who, in turn, would sabotage transportation and communication facilities up and down the coast.

"Blessent mon coeur d'une languer monotone. (Wound my heart with a monotonous languor).
Coded radio broadcast to the French resistance, indicating the invasion would take place in 48 hours.

"Under the command of General Eisenhower, Allied naval forces supported by strong air forces began landing Allied armies this morning on the coast of France."
Radio broadcast to the people of Britain, June 6th, 1944.

The Airborne Assault

The wind, which was making choppy waves in the Channel, had its impact on the paratroopers. On the eastern flank the 6th Airborne Division (which included the 1st Canadian Parachute Battalion) was scattered well beyond its drop zone between the Orne and Dives Rivers east of Caen. Nevertheless, the division managed to seize most of their objectives and by early morning the paratroopers were working desperately to make their area into a defensive zone against an anticipated German armoured attack. Thus while the bridges over the Orne River and Canal were seized, those over the Dives were demolished. The numerous deep drainage ditches and inundated fields would make it difficult for tanks to penetrate. Behind them, other fields were cleared of poles in preparation for a brigade arriving by gliders on the afternoon of D-Day. Landing in the midst of enemy positions in the dark, the paratroopers were engaged in fighting enemy-held positions all day and no group was happier to see British commandos when they arrived to reinforce their positions later that day.

Some 70 km to the west, on the American sector of the invasion front, two US Airborne Divisions - the 82nd and 101st - were landing shortly after midnight. Their objectives were somewhat similar to the British in that rivers, canals and flooded areas were involved. Directly behind "Utah" Beach, where the 4th US Infantry Division was to land, there was a two-km-wide lagoon. Four causeways crossed this stretch of water which provided exits from the beach. Paratroopers were to seize these causeways, cut the road and railway heading northwest to Cherbourg, capture or destroy certain bridges over nearby rivers and form a defensive ring inland from "Utah" Beach until the seaborne troops arrived.

The area to be covered by the parachute and glider troops was much larger than their British counterparts. Like them, strong winds, heavy anti-aircraft fire and difficulties in navigation resulted in the troops being widely scattered. The 101st for example, were dispersed in territory measuring 3.5 km long and 21 km wide. It took hours, in some cases days, before companies and battalions could be united. Meanwhile small mixed groups had to attack the numerous objectives the divisions had been assigned. Many had landed in inundated or swampy areas and were drowned. By daybreak, however, the majority of the tasks allotted to them had been accomplished, frequently by small groups of paratroopers benefitting from the surprise of their assault and the confusion of the defenders.

Although the wide dispersal of the British and American paratroopers made it very difficult for them to carry out their planned attacks, it gave the Germans the impression that the airborne assault was on a much larger scale. Parachutists seemed to be landing everywhere. To add to their confusion the Allies used "dummy" parachutists scattered over a wide area. These dummies contained a mechanical contrivance which, when they struck the ground, gave off the sound of rifle fire and explosives, much like the sound of a string of firecrackers. Intelligence reports reaching German divisional headquarters made it hard for the commanders to decide where the main thrust of the attack was aimed. At the same time, on a higher level, reports were being received about a large force approaching the Pas de Calais. Operation "Fortitude" was in full swing. It was two hours after the first paratroopers arrived before the German Seventh Army, responsible for the defence of Normandy, was placed on the highest invasion alert. Another three hours were to pass before Rommel's headquarters were told that ships were concentrating off the coast of Normandy. Between 5:30 and 6:00 a.m., with assault craft in the water and heading for the beaches, the naval bombardment of the coastal defences roared out from naval ships. H Hour had arrived.

"Along the whole 50 mile front the land was rocked by successive explosions as the shells of ships' guns tore holes in fortifications and tons of bombs rained on them from the skies. Through billowing smoke and falling debris defenders crouching in this scene of devastation would soon discern faintly hundreds of ships and assault craft ominously closing the

shore... the soldiers borne forward to attack were thrilled by the spectacle of Allied power that was displayed around them on every hand."
L.F. Ellis. British Official Historian.

The American Landings

Utah Beach

The tides in the English Channel were from west to east and, as a result, American troops started their run-in before the British. Furthermost to the west was "Utah" Beach where the American 4th Infantry Division was to land. As the assault craft began their long approach to the shore, the men could hear the naval shells whistling overhead. The noise of the bombardment was increased by the roar of both heavy and light bombers flying overhead to add their weight to the navy's gunfire. Going in with the infantry were the D-D Tanks and special troops to demolish a clear path through the beach obstacles.

Owing to the early morning mist, the smoke, the current and the difficulty to distinguish land marks, the assaulting troops landed about a mile east of their intended area. Fortunately the troops met little opposition on the beaches and by mid-morning men and vehicles were moving inland across two of the causeways over the lagoon to meet with members of the 101st and 82nd Airborne Divisions. Behind them more waves of troops and vehicles were landing and as the other causeways were opened and additional troops pounded in, the 4th Division steadily pressed forward bringing welcome relief, especially in the form of heavy weapons and tanks, to the parachutists. By the end of the day the assaulting seaborne troops had lost less than 200 men.

Omaha Beach

On "Omaha" Beach the situation was far different. Behind this beach the land rose steeply with only four exits leading to the plateau above. These were mined and contained belts of barbed wire. Their approaches were covered by enemy fire. From their emplacements along the high ground, the enemy could pour rifle, machine-gun and mortar fire down on the beaches as well as artillery fire from inland batteries.

"Two kinds of people are staying on this beach, the dead and those about to die. Now let's get the Hell out of here!"
George A. Taylor, Colonel, United States Army

Almost from the beginning things began to go wrong. Many of the D-D Tanks launched over three miles from the beach were swamped and sank. Despite the naval and air bombardment there were numerous enemy bunkers and fortifications undamaged by the fire and when the infantry assault boats were only a few hundred yards from shore they met with a withering hail of machine-gun, mortar and shell fire. Moreover, unknown to the Allies until the last minute, an additional German Division had been moved into the area so their strength was much stronger than anticipated. Some of the landing craft landed some distance from their planned position and the clearing of beach obstacles was delayed. Men raced across the beach seeking some shelter at the base of the cliffs. Casualties mounted as more waves arrived to add to the confusion on the beach where for some hours any attempt to move inland seemed doomed to failure. Gradually, however, individuals and groups began to fight their way up the gullies and in desperate fighting, pushed the enemy away from the cliffs. By the end of the day the division was two or three km inland on a five km front. It had suffered 2,500 casualties. Only a limited number of tanks and vehicles had managed to move off the beach. For a while there was some doubt if the narrow beachhead could survive a determined German counter-attack.

The British - Canadian Beaches

The British-Canadian sector of the Normandy coast stretched 25 km from Port-en-Bessin, the boundary with the Americans, to Cabourg at the mouth of the Dives River. In this sector these assault beaches had been chosen codenamed "Gold", "Juno", and "Sword" where the 50th (Northumbrian), 3rd Canadian and the British 3rd Infantry Divisions respectively, would land, each supported by tanks and special forces. In all more than 70,000 troops would assault the beaches, including 15,000 Canadians along the 8 km stretch of beach known as "Juno".

Protecting this sector was the enemy's 716th Division. Its eight infantry battalions had prepared defensive positions ranging from slit trenches to concrete bunkers. These units were strengthened by 90 guns of

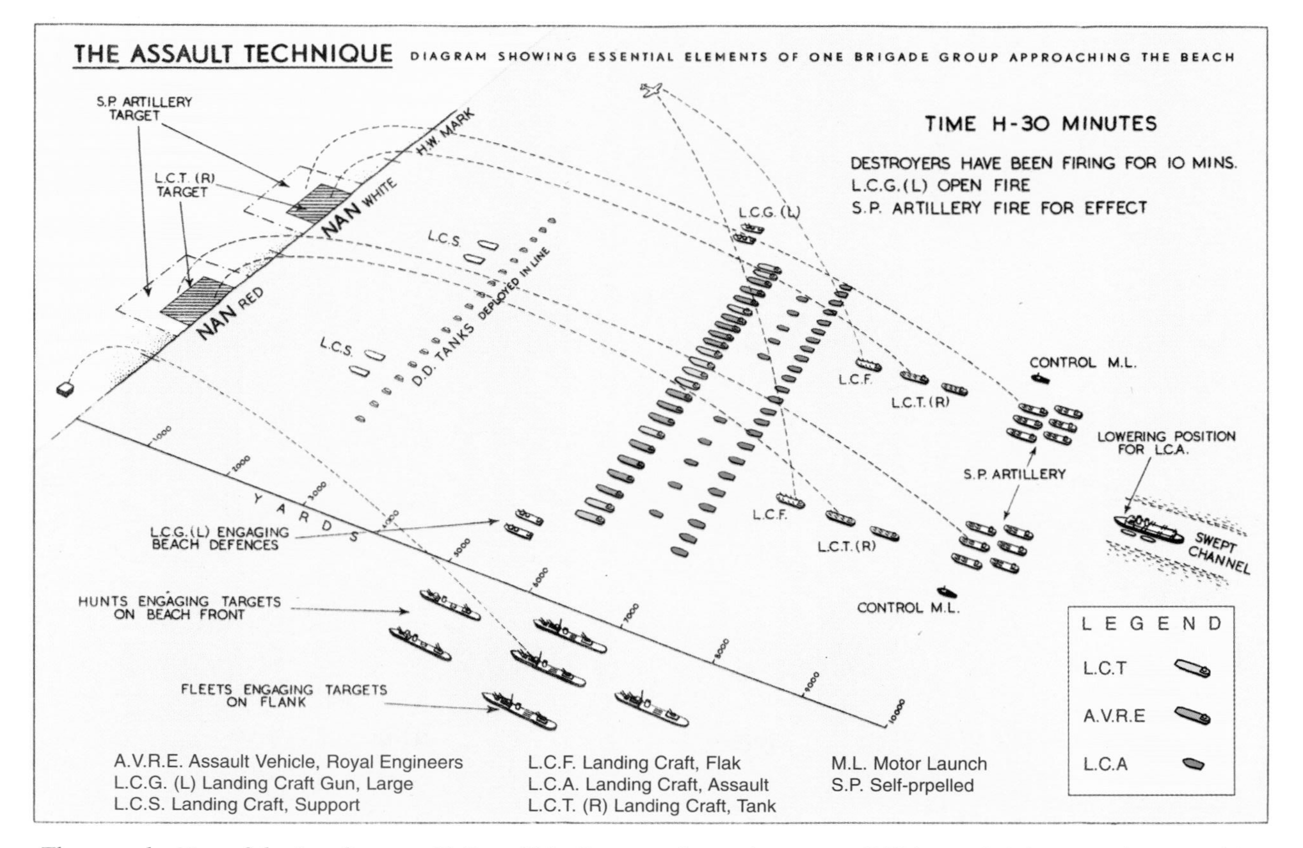

The complexities of the Landings on D-Day. This diagram shows the responsibilities and tight control required for success. NAN Red and White were the beaches where the North Shore Regiment and the Queen's Own landed.

up to 88-mm calibre, nearly 50 mortars, and between 400 and 500 machine-guns. In addition, in the coastal belt, there were 22 batteries of field, medium and heavy artillery containing a further 90 guns and some 40 heavy anti-tank guns. Behind the coastal belt, in the rear area, were five more battalions of infantry or panzer grenadiers, five batteries of medium and heavy guns, 34 self-propelled 88-mm guns and additional anti-tank units in the process of formation. These defences and fortifications, most protected by mine-fields and barbed wire, were formidable even though the 716th Division itself was not classified as first rate.

What concerned the Allied planners more was that there were two German armoured formations nearby. The closest was the 21st Panzer Division near Caen, 16 km away, and the 12th SS Panzer Division a few km further inland. The D-Day objectives on the British-Canadian front were to seize Bayeux and Caen and the road and railway routes between them. Armoured columns were to try to strike even further inland if possible. This would give needed depth to the invading forces and provide a cushion for the anticipated armoured counter-attacks.

The strong winds and choppy waves made things difficult for the landing craft as they lined up 10 km off shore for the run in to "Gold" Beach. To avoid their being swamped, the D-D Tanks were taken directly to the beach. Splashing through four-foot waves and a wind which pushed the tide higher up the beach than expected, the first wave touched down at 7:30 a.m. Fortunately many of the D-D Tanks and other specialized armour landed within them and were able to batter many of the concrete bunkers the air and naval bombardment had missed. Resistance on the coast varied. In some places it was very stiff, on others only modest. The beach obstacles took their toll. Of 16 landing craft carrying the 47th Royal Marine Commandos, for example, four were lost and eleven were damaged. Despite their rough landing, this elite group was soon on its way towards Putot-en-Bessin to link up with the Americans.

Aided by the D-D Tanks and close support from the destroyers off shore, German coastal defences were overcome. By 9:30 a.m. some of the battalions and an additional two brigades landing at 11:00 a.m. were soon plunging forward and by evening they had patrols entering Bayeux and beyond 10 km from the coast. Units from the German 352nd Division, which the Americans encountered on "Omaha" Beach, were met and pushed back. It was a long, hard fight. Fortunately, here as on the other

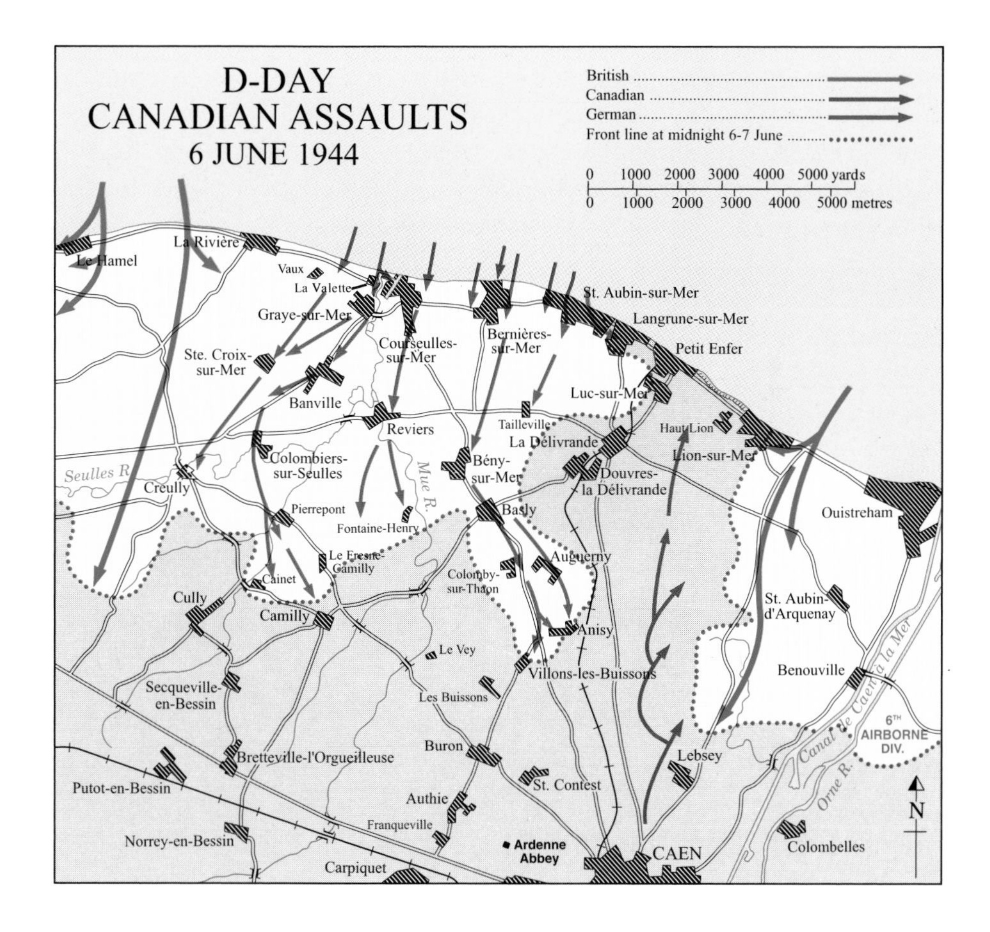
D-DAY
CANADIAN ASSAULTS
6 JUNE 1944
British
Canadian
German
Front line at midnight 6-7 June
0 1000 2000 3000 4000 5000 yards
0 1000 2000 3000 4000 5000 metres
Le Hamel
La Rivière
Vaux
La Valette
Graye-sur-Mer
Ste. Croix-sur-Mer
Courseulles-sur-Mer
Banville
Bernières-sur-Mer
St. Aubin-sur-Mer
Langrune-sur-Mer
Petit Enfer
Luc-sur-Mer
Tailleville
La Délivrande
Haut Lion
Lion-sur-Mer
Reviers
Seulles R.
Creully
Colombiers-sur-Seulles
Mue R.
Bény-sur-Mer
Douvres-la Délivrande
Ouistreham
Pierrepont
Fontaine-Henry
Basly
Le Fresne-Camilly
Cainet
Colomby-sur-Thaon
Anguerny
Cully
Camilly
St. Aubin-d'Arquenay
Anisy
Le Vey
Villons-les-Buissons
Benouville
Secqueville-en-Bessin
Les Buissons
6TH AIRBORNE DIV.
Canal de Caen à la Mer
Buron
Lebsey
Bretteville-l'Orgueilleuse
Putot-en-Bessin
St. Contest
Orne R.
Authie
N
Franqueville
Norrey-en-Bessin
Ardenne Abbey
CAEN
Colombelles
Carpiquet

beaches, there was only one brief attack by two German fighter aircraft during the entire day. The Allies had complete control of the air.

Sword Beach

"Sword" Beach, where the British 3rd Infantry Division landed, was hammered by naval guns somewhat longer than the other beaches since German defences there were more numerous. Most of the D-D Tanks arrived just before the infantry splashed ashore. The higher than expected tides together with landing craft casualties among the beach obstacles caused the same congestion of vehicles on the foreshore being experienced by the Canadians. Several exits were made from the beach and two hours after the landing elements were about two kilometres inland on a narrow front. Commando units came ashore to connect with the 6th Airborne Division east of the Orne River while another fought all day to clear the beachhead westward and make contact with the Canadians.

Once several km inland the troops pushed steadily but cautiously towards Caen. By four o'clock the leading elements were seven kilometres inland at Bienville but a little further on they met with strong resistance from the 21st Panzer Division. The attack lost its momentum. The reinforcing brigade had been held up by the weather and when it was forming up for its advance, the brigade Commander and some of his staff were struck by a mortar bomb. The weight of the division was needed to get into Caen and this was lacking. It would be another month before the British and Canadians could fight their way into the city.

The Canadian Landing - Juno Beach

Order of Battle - June 6th, 1944,
3rd Canadian Division - First Wave - 7:45 am
Left beach - Infantry- Queens Own Rifles of Canada, The North Shore Regiment, Le Regiment de la Chaudiere (reserve)
Armour - The Fort Garry Horse (D-D Tanks)
Right beach - Infantry - Royal Winnipeg Rifles, The Regina Rifles, The Canadian Scottish (reserve)
Armour - 1st Hussars (D-D Tanks)

D-Day by Tom Wood (CWM 10558)

"It was becoming light and in the first glimmer of dawn we saw the ships massed around.. Explosions rumbled as the bombing continued and the heavy naval guns fired several salvos... The wind had gone considerably and a haze misted the sea... Just before six, we saw the French coast, lying low and dark against a slate-grey sky... Lines of assault craft, lashing through the sea, passed by our ship. You could see the infantrymen and sappers crouched in their craft, gripping their weapons, their battle-dress soaked already by the spray. These were the heroic first-wave troops, going now to the battle on the beaches."
Ross Munro, Canadian War Correspondent.

On "Juno" Beach the Canadians came in under a canopy of fire from the naval ships which threw up clouds of dust and smoke along the coast. As they closed in to the beach, rocket and artillery fire from special landing craft supported them as they neared the beach obstacles. Shortly before 8 a.m. the infantry and D-D Tanks were splashing ashore. As with "Gold" Beach, there were many emplacements which had not been damaged by the bombardment. Although a fair number of the D-D Tanks were lost to enemy fire and to the mixed beach obstacles, most had made it to the shore where they rendered invaluable help, together with the AVREs, in subduing the concrete fortifications along the coast.

As the tide rose higher, the beach became narrower until the congestion of men and vehicles was eased as exits were blasted in the sea wall and the fighting moved further inland.

"Their (the German's) camouflage was perfect and it was no wonder we did not see them earlier... There was only one course of action, and to a man the platoon rushed the enemy positions. It was a bitter encounter with much hand-to-hand fighting."
Anonymous Officer, The Canadian Scottish.

"D-D tanks began to cruise up and down the beach engaging machine-gun nests. At first the fire was so intense that the crew commanders had difficulty in locating the targets... permitting the infantry to sweep over the dunes to begin their push inland..."
Official History of The Royal Winnipeg Rifles.

Making smoke off Juno Sector, Normandy, June 1944 by A.G. Broomfield

(CWM 14369)

Pushing Inland

In the fields beyond the beach there were numerous battles to be fought even while conflict continued along the beach. Villages and farmhouses had thick stone walls and the Germans made good use of them. Minefields and anti-tank guns took their toll as the Canadians pushed inland. By noon, when the infantry had thrust almost four km inland, "B" Squadron of the 1st Hussars had only ten tanks still operational out of nineteen it had launched in the attack. Some of the infantry carried bicycles ashore to get inland quicker. Behind them, on the beaches, men worked feverishly to get vehicles towing artillery or carrying mortars and medium machine-guns through the beach exits and on to support the infantry, steadily advancing towards Pierreport, Beny-sur-Mer and Colomby-sur-Thaon.

Order of Battle, June 6th, 1944
3rd Canadian Division - Second Wave - 11:00 am
Infantry - North Nova Scotia Highlanders, Highland Light Infantry, Stormont, Dundas and Glengarry Highlanders.
Armour - The Sherbrooke Fusiliers (Tanks)

By late afternoon the reserve brigade had landed and was moving inland. Resistance was stiffening as it came closer to Caen but by nightfall the leading elements were over eight km inland while one group of the 1st Hussars had reached the main Caen-Bayeux road. It was well beyond the infantry and had to withdraw from its exposed position. Even at that, the Canadians had fought their way further from the beach than any other allied assault division.

Between the beaches and the furthest patrols inland there were still enemy fortified posts holding out. Scattered fighting would continue during the night. On the Canadian right contact had been made with the British 50th Division but on the left there was still a considerable gap between the Canadians and the British assault division headed for Caen.

The German Response

The most pressing priority for the Allies at the end of D-Day was to consolidate their gains and ensure that the anticipated German counter-attack was defeated. On the German side the Allied attack had come as a complete surprise. The naval and air bombardment during the night and early dawn had disrupted communications. Constant air attacks during the day, in addition to the sabotage strikes by the French Resistance, made it difficult to obtain firm information about the scope of the Allied landings. The scattered drops of the three airborne divisions added more confusion to the reports coming in to their headquarters. Deception measures in the Pas de Calais area made the enemy believe that the Normandy landings were a feint and thus led to poor strategic planning on their part.

"I therefore consider that an attempt be made, using every possible expedient, to beat off the enemy landing on the coast..."
Erwin Rommel, Commander of the German's Coastal Defences

The German Seventh Army had the responsibility of defending the Normandy coast. Its Commander was away from his headquarters when the parachutists started to land around midnight. The headquarters did not issue an alert about a possible invasion until 1:40 a.m. The 21st Panzer Division was ordered to operate against the 6th Airborne Division before dawn but it received no direct orders to move as a division until about 8:30 a.m. It was attacking the airborne troops east of the Orne River when, in mid-morning, it was ordered to come west of the river to defeat Caen. It blunted the British 3rd Division's attack on that city and it also managed to thrust a small armoured column between the British and Canadian divisions. The German tanks reached the coast near Lion-sur-Mer in the evening but it turned back when gliders from the Air Landing Brigade, flying in to reinforce the 6th Airborne Division, swept overhead.

Casualties on the first day of battle were about half of what had been anticipated. The Americans had suffered more than 6,600 killed and wounded while the British-Canadian assault lost more than 3,000. On Juno beach Canada had lost 1,074 men, including 335 dead. Two thirds of the dead were soldiers killed in the first-wave.

"And that very first night we stated burying our dead. When you start burying your buddies, you want to quit. You think what's the use of going on. But we did."
Angus Kearns, Private, The Canadian Scottish.

Men of The Stormont, Dundas and Glengarry Highlanders landing at Bernieres-sur-Mer, June 6th, 1944. (NAC PA 122765)

Canadian wounded waiting for evacuation from Juno Beach, June 6th, 1944. (NAC PA 132384)

"...the wheat field had once been like any wheatfield back home. Now it was torn with shell holes and everywhere you could see the pale, upturned faces of the dead... We dug narrow graves and lowered them to rest... I blessed a group of graves and said the burial prayers. I often thought that somewhere a mother, a father, a wife, a sister or brother still hoped and prayed."
R.M. Hickey, Padre, The North Shore Regiment.

By nightfall, across the entire Allied front some 75,215 British and Canadian and about 57,500 American troops had been landed on the shores of Normandy, while 7,900 British and Canadian and 15,500 American airborne troops had landed from the sky. In the British-Canadian sector, despite the difficulties from underwater obstacles and direct fire, over 6,000 vehicles (including 900 tanks and armoured vehicles) had been put ashore, together with some 240 field guns, 80 light anti-aircraft guns, and over 40,000 tonnes of stores. This was but the beginning of the invasion.

D Plus One; Wednesday, June 7th, 1944

Counter-Thrust

The 12th SS Panzer Division, which occupied a large area around Evreux, 80 km away, was the next nearest German armoured division to the Normandy coast. It had been alerted at 4 a.m. but it, together with the Panzer Lehr and 17th SS Panzer Grenadier Divisions, could not be moved without the express approval of Hitler. Despite the request from von Rundstedt at 4:45 a.m. for their release this was not granted. Hitler and his senior generals were still not sure if this was the major landing. It was not until mid-afternoon that these divisions were released for operations. With Allied aircraft dominating the skies, movement by tanks or vehicles by road invited ferocious attacks. The 12th SS Panzer Division did not make its presence felt until June 7th.

The first Allied assault division to run into German tank opposition was the British 3rd Division. When, on June 7th, it attempted to move closer to Caen, its advance on Lebisey was met and defeated by the 12th SS Panzer Division which had just come into the line. This German division was one of the elite formations available to Rommel. Its soldiers were

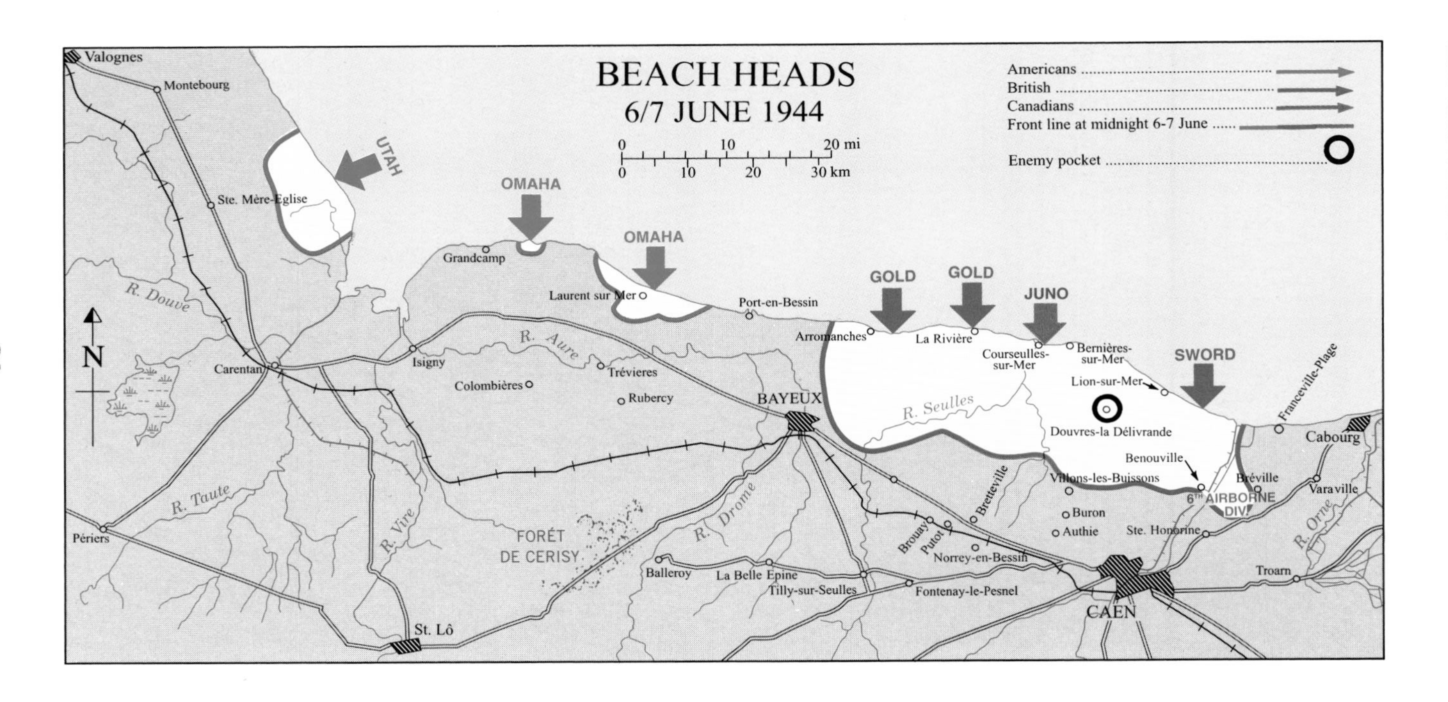
BEACH HEADS
6/7 JUNE 1944
0 10 20 mi
0 10 20 30 km
Americans
British
Canadians
Front line at midnight 6-7 June
Enemy pocket
UTAH
OMAHA
OMAHA
GOLD
GOLD
JUNO
SWORD
6TH AIRBORNE DIV.
Valognes
Montebourg
Ste. Mère-Eglise
Carentan
Isigny
Grandcamp
Laurent sur Mer
Port-en-Bessin
Arromanches
La Rivière
Courseulles-sur-Mer
Bernières-sur-Mer
Lion-sur-Mer
Douvres-la Délivrande
Benouville
Villons-les-Buissons
Buron
Authie
Ste. Honorine
CAEN
Bréville
Franceville-Plage
Cabourg
Varaville
Troarn
R. Orne
Bretteville
Norrey-en-Bessin
Putot
Brouay
Fontenay-le-Pesnel
Tilly-sur-Seulles
La Belle Epine
Balleroy
BAYEUX
R. Seulles
R. Drome
R. Aure
Trévieres
Rubercy
Colombières
FORÊT DE CERISY
St. Lô
R. Vire
R. Taute
R. Douve
Périers
N

young men, most of them in their late teens and all imbued with Nazi ideals. Most of the non-commissioned officers, as well as most of the officers, were experienced veterans, many of whom had been hardened and brutalized by fighting the Russians on the Eastern Front.

On the British right, but still separated by a gap, was the 3rd Canadian Infantry Division. Its front had been fairly quiet during the night but it was to push on to its D-Day objective - the Caen-Bayeux railway line - early on the following morning. The Canadian battalions of the 7th Brigade made good progress. Enemy resistance was soon overcome and by midday the leading unit could claim it was the first in the Second British Army to reach its D-Day target.

The 9th Canadian Infantry Brigade led the advance on the Canadian left. This brigade had landed on the beaches behind schedule but it had moved well inland by darkness. Led by the North Nova Scotia Highlanders, the brigade was to strike south towards the Carpiquet airport on the outskirts of Caen. Accompanied by tanks from the Sherbrooke Fusiliers, the Highlanders advanced three km before running into stubborn resistance at Buron, half way to their objective. Enemy shell and mortar fire was made more aggravating since the unit was beyond the range of its own artillery. While one company of infantry and some tanks fought to clear Buron, the remainder of the unit by-passed the village and entered Authie about a mile further south. With each passing hour the enemy's fire increased. It was the prelude to the counter-attack of the 12th SS Panzer Division. Led by Colonel Kurt Meyer, who had three infantry and one tank battalions under his command, the Canadians were soon involved in a desperate swirling battle.

"In the square in Authie, laughing SS troops propped a dead Canadian against the wall of a house, put a German helmet on his head, a cigarette in his mouth, a beer bottle in the crook of his arm."
W.R. Bird, Historian of the North Nova Scotia Highlanders.

As the fighting progressed Meyer thrust more men and tanks into the battle. Authie was partially surrounded and its defenders either killed, wounded or taken prisoner. A few escaped north through the shellfire to Buron which was also being attacked by infantry and tanks from the south and west. By late afternoon the area between Authie, Buron and further north to Les Buissons was receiving the undivided attention of Colonel Meyer's tanks, artillery and infantry. The Canadian left flank was open as the British had not advanced far enough to protect it. From a tower in the medieval Abbey of Ardenne Meyer had an excellent view of the battlefield. His units fought hard and eventually occupied Buron but at a considerable cost. At times there was hand to hand fighting and German and Canadian tanks battled until nightfall until the fields were littered with them in various stages of destruction. When Meyer tried to push beyond Buron, Canadian field guns were within range and hammered the enemy to a halt. The 8th Brigade formed a strong defensive line which halted any further attempt on their part to reach the beaches. That night each side licked its wounds but on the following day, with additional forces coming into the line, the 12th SS would attack again. In the ferocious fighting at Authie the North Nova Scotia Highlanders lost 242 men, including 84 dead and 128 prisoners.

D Plus Two; Thursday, June 8th, 1944

On the morning of June 8th the 7th Canadian Infantry Brigade holding the right flank of the divisional front came under increasing fire from the 12th SS Panzer Division. The Regina Rifle Regiment, digging in on their D-Day objective at Norrey-en-Bessin, managed to beat off their opponents but at Putot-en-Bessin the Royal Winnipeg Rifles were being battered as the enemy swarmed around the village. With ammunition running low and in danger of being cut off, the Winnipegs had to release their grip on Putot. The tanks of the 1st Hussars had suffered heavy losses and calls for help for armoured support could not be met at that time.

"The ensuing battle was horrendous with the tanks circling our solid stone house and surrounding high stone walls. The night was lit by the burning barns at the farm and the tanks overran one platoon in the orchard behind the north wall crushing anti-tank guns, carriers and soldiers."
Gordon Brown, Major, The Regina Rifles.

Should Putot be lost the Regina Rifles would be left in a very exposed position with both flanks open to the constant pressures from Meyer's

A destroyed Panther tank on the main street in Bretteville.The tank was put out of action by the Regina Rifles using PIAT bombs. (NAC PA 130149)

Allied anti-aircraft fire over the Normandy bridgehead, June 1944. (PAC PA 138754)

26th SS Panzer Regiment.The Canadian Scottish was about three km behind the two forward rifle units and early in the evening it was ordered to recapture Putot. Lieutenant-Colonel Fred Cabeldu had only two hours before he crossed the start-line. He had to gather his companies, arrange for a creeping artillery barrage, liaise with the 1st Hussars for some tank support, arrange a preliminary smoke screen and have everything coordinated for crossing the start-line at 8:30 p.m. For a unit which had been in action only two days it was a remarkable task. Nevertheless the Canadian Scottish with its supporting elements went into the attack on time. By nightfall, after savage fighting, Putot was again in Canadian hands. The unit suffered 125 casualties in this action, almost all killed or wounded.

Murder

It was some time later that the Canadians found out that several dozen of the prisoners captured by the 12th SS Panzer Division during the fighting for Buron and Putot were killed in cold blood. This was not an isolated criminal act. By the end of the Normandy campaign there is documented proof that 156 Canadian prisoners had been murdered by members of this division, a measure of the ruthlessness with which they waged war.

"They looked like babies and fought like mad bastards."
Anonymous Canadian soldier commenting on the 12th SS, Hitler Youth Division. The unit was made up principally of 18 year-olds and fought with fanaticism and barbarity throughout the Normandy campaign. Between the Canadians and the 12th SS the fighting was always vicious. Taking prisoners was considered optional.

Despite their desperate attacks, both the 21st and 12th SS Panzer Divisions were unable to crack the British-Canadian lines. They had been committed piecemeal in order to defend Caen. This city was a hub of road, rail and canal transportation routes. Its capture, the Germans felt, would provide the hinge for the Allied forces in Normandy to swing northwards to connect with another Allied invasion force the Germans expected to land in the Pas de Calais area. Thus when the third German armoured division - the Panzer Lehr - arrived, it was sent into the line against the British 50th Division on the Canadian right. Owing to the pressure on their front

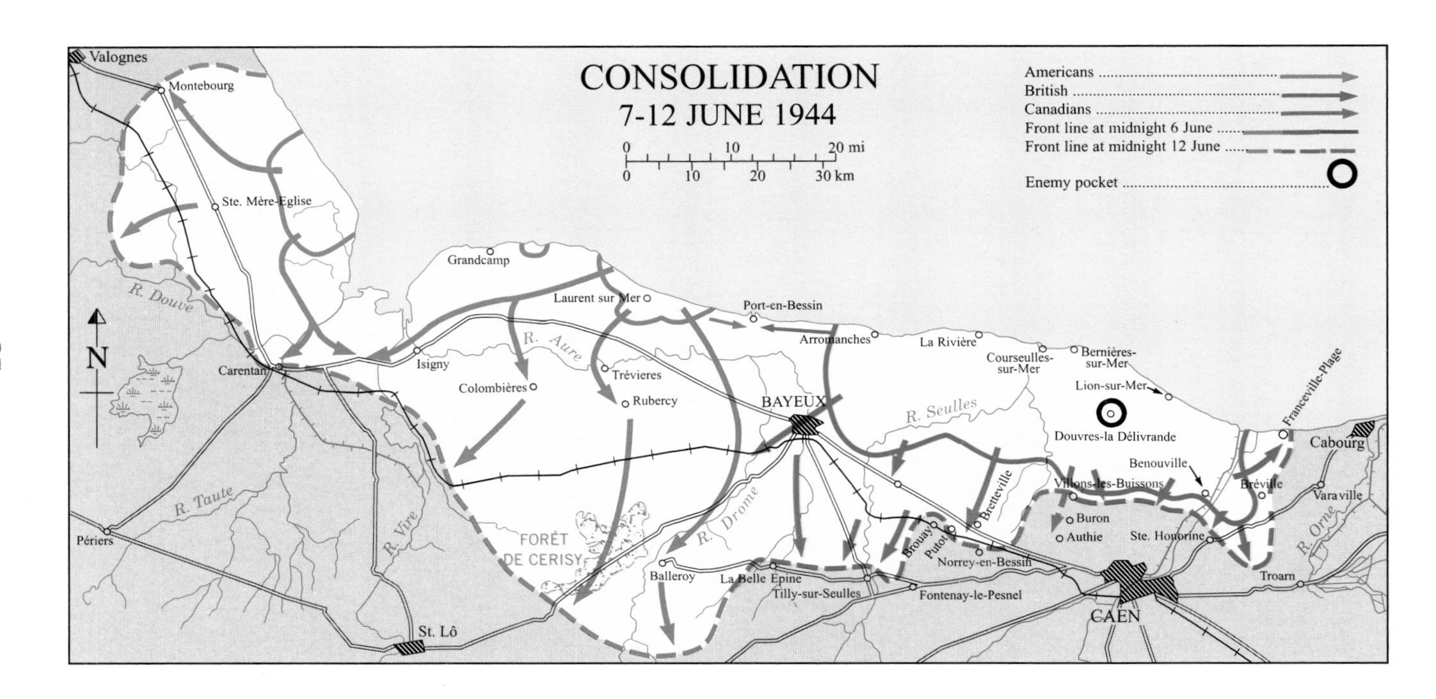
CONSOLIDATION
7-12 JUNE 1944
0 10 20 mi
0 10 20 30 km
Americans
British
Canadians
Front line at midnight 6 June
Front line at midnight 12 June
Enemy pocket
N
Valognes
Montebourg
Ste. Mère-Eglise
Grandcamp
R. Douve
Carentan
Isigny
R. Aure
Laurent sur Mer
Port-en-Bessin
Arromanches
La Rivière
Courseulles-sur-Mer
Bernières-sur-Mer
Lion-sur-Mer
Trévieres
Colombières
Rubercy
BAYEUX
R. Seulles
Douvres-la Délivrande
Franceville-Plage
Cabourg
Benouville
Villons-les-Buissons
Bréville
Varaville
Bretteville
Buron
Authie
Ste. Honorine
R. Orne
R. Taute
Périers
R. Vire
FORÊT DE CERISY
R. Drome
Balleroy
La Belle Epine
Tilly-sur-Seulles
Brouay
Putot
Norrey-en-Bessin
Fontenay-le-Pesnel
CAEN
Troarn
St. Lô

in this area the Panzer Lehr, already hard hit by Allied air power route to the battlefront, was also committed piecemeal. As a result instead of having a mailed fist of three panzer divisions to smash through the Allied defences to the sea, Rommel had to use them in a defensive role.

By June 8th, when the Panzer Lehr was coming into the area, the Allied position had greatly improved. The British 50th Division had captured Bayeux and had pushed slightly south of it. The capture of Port-en-Bessin connected the 50th Division with the American forces on "Omaha" Beach which, after their harsh struggle to gain a foothold, were reinforced and pushed well inland towards St. Lo. Further west, the two airborne divisions and the American 4th Division had difficulty fighting but had managed to seize an area some 11 km deep and 12 km wide. The two American beachheads, however, had not joined up. Carentan, a major town with a network of rivers and inundated areas around it, stood in the gap between the two American forces and was proving to be a hard nut to crack. It was not until June 10th that all the beaches were joined.

Securing the Beachhead

During this period each side worked desperately to build up their forces. On the Allied side two huge artificial harbours had been constructed in Great Britain called Mulberry "A" and Mulberry "B". The former would be constructed for the Americans near St. Laurent, the latter for the British at Arromanches. A breakwater would be created by sunken block ships and the construction of an outer sea wall made up of huge concrete caissons, some three stories high, which would be towed across the channel and sunk in their proper position. Inside this shelter floating roadways, called whales, would lead to a pier. The harbour was designed to take "Liberty" ships which had a 26-foot draught and the floating roadways had to engineered to take into account the 23-foot tides on the Normandy coast. It was hoped that both "Mulberries" would be in operation a week after D-Day but in practice it was some two weeks before both harbours were operating at full capacity. Meanwhile the follow-up divisions with their tanks, trucks, ammunition, stores and a multitude of military equipment had to be landed over the beaches. Each division of approximately 15,000 men required some 630 tonnes of supplies every day to maintain its men and vehicles. The logistics involved in bringing over and supplying additional formations in Normandy could never be forgotten by the Allied commanders when planning their battles.

For the Germans, bringing infantry and armoured divisions to reinforce their front in Normandy was no easy task. With Allied control of the air, movement of German vehicles and tanks by road or rail offered immediate tempting targets to the fighter-bombers. Only at night could the enemy move his formations without being attacked. Even at that the rail and road network with its bridges, tunnels and marshalling yards was constantly hammered and movement on them delayed. This more than balanced the Allied build-up which was behind the planned schedule. Moreover, still believing a second invasion was coming in the Pas de Calais, the Germans brought in divisions from further afield, thus exposing them to air attack.

On the American front it took several days before the two airborne divisions were able to collect their scattered battalions in a coherent front. On June 7th"Utah" Beach had expanded to a beachhead 11 km deep and 12 km wide. Reinforcements pouring through "Omaha" Beach had greatly improved the position there. With three divisions available, the Americans were able to make an all out attack on Carentan. Its capture on June 12th linked up both American beachheads so that by that date the Allies had a lodgement area all along the invasion coast with its deepest point some 40 km inland.

In the British sector congestion on the beaches and difficulties encountered in creating sufficient exits from the area had slowed the disembarkation of the two follow-up divisions - the British 7th Armoured and the 51st Highland Divisions. The former was to go to the Bayeux area, the latter across the Orne to support the 6th Airborne and 3rd British Infantry Divisions. General Montgomery had planned to use these two formations to make a pincer movement on Caen but the attack by both met stiff resistance. Panzer Lehr Division was nearby and when the 7th Armoured Division struck south to capture Tilly-sur-Seulles and beyond, it could hold on to only the edge of the village by the end of the day. The appearance of a new German armoured formation on its front, the 2nd Panzer, made Montgomery believe the Germans were preparing the long-awaited armoured counter-stroke which, indeed, they were.

Rommel had given this task to General von Schweppenburg, commanding Panzer Group West. Unfortunately for him, his headquarters had been located. It was hit by bombers which destroyed the headquarters, wounded the Commander and killed or wounded most of the staff officers. The planned counter-offensive was called off and with it any hope of pushing the Allies back into the sea faded.

The End of The First Phase

By the night of June 11th/12th the Allies had landed 326,547 men, 54,186 vehicles and 95,000 tonnes of stores ashore on the continent. By this time, too, the course of the coming campaign was beginning to shape up. The original plan to seize Caen and the area south-east of it had been frustrated by the 21st Panzer Division. Within the next few days the 12th SS Panzer Division, Panzer Lehr and the 2nd Panzer Division had come up to the British-Canadian front and had been thrown into the line to stop any further advances on that front. So far no armoured divisions had appeared on the American front which allowed the Americans to continue to fight their way across the Cotentin Peninsula. This was no easy task, but it would have been much more difficult had German armour opposed them.

This development, in turn, caused Montgomery to adjust his overall plan. By continuing to hit hard and continuously in the east he hoped to continue to attract German panzer divisions to the British-Canadian front and away from the Americans. This would allow the latter to gain more territory and prepare the way for a break-out from the lodgement area. This was to take place at the end of July but it involved much bitter fighting before the forces were in position to attack.

The severity of the fighting in Normandy during the first six days can be measured in the casualty rates. On D-Day itself, to use the Canadians as an example, an estimated 1,074 men were killed and wounded. At that, this was less than anticipated. After six days in action the Canadians battle casualties totalled 2,831, including 1,017 killed. By the time the campaign was over in late August, the Canadian casualty figure was 18,444 of which 5,021 were fatal. From a regimental perspective one might use the Canadian Scottish Regiment as an example. On D-Day it landed with a strength of about 800 all ranks. By August 21st it had suffered 627 casualties, one third of whom were killed in action.

Conclusion

By nightfall of June 6th, 1944 it was apparent the invasion had been a success. Few of the D-Day objectives were in Allied hands but these were optimistic when the plans had been made. Great breaches had been made in the so-called Atlantic Wall. Some of the fortifications along the coastal region were to hold out for several days until they were pounded into submission. Along the entire front, however, infantry, tanks, artillery, engineers and other units had fought their way inland. They now faced the tasks of connecting the beachheads to form a bridgehead and then expanding that into a lodgement area. It was hoped that on the following day another two divisions would arrive and, within a week some fifteen divisions would be ashore. They needed room, thus expanding the lodgement area was vital.

The assault on the coast of Normandy was a prelude of greater battles to come. It was an unforgettable experience for every sailor, soldier and airman who took part in it. Its success was a remarkable achievement considering the risks involved.

"In the history of the Second World War the Normandy D-Day is notable for Canada, not merely as the date of a supreme military achievement... The day was further brightened by an unusual conjunction. For once all three of the Canadian services were fought together. The 3rd Division held the centre stage; but overhead the Canadian bombers of No. 6 Group and the fighter squadrons in No.83 played their parts... while Canadian minesweepers helped to clear the way across the turbulent Channel, and Canadian naval guns helped to beat down the enemy's defences... the 3rd Division was landed by craft of the Royal Canadian Navy. In the Canadian calendar this Sixth of June, so full of consequences for the cause of freedom, deserves to be 'marked evermore with white'."
C.P. Stacey, Official Canadian Historian.

A sad legacy of D-Day: The returned letter to Wendell Clark from his family. The letter was stamped "Reported Missing", and returned to the distraught sender.

The losses on D-Day were much lower than expected, only 335 dead. Amongst the missing, later listed as dead, was Regimental Sergeant Major Wendell Clark of the 1st Canadian Parachute Regiment. Clark went missing on June 6th when he parachuted into Normandy. His body was found after the war. Wendell James Clark, of Ottawa, is now buried in Ranville War Cemetery, France.

(Dan Charbonneau)

Bibliography - Suggested Reading

Victory in the West, Vol.1: The Battle of Normandy. By Major L.F.Ellis. HMSO, 1962

The Victory Campaign, Vol. III of the Official History of the Canadian Army in the Second World War. by Colonel C.P.Stacey. Queens Printer, 1960

Cross Channel Attack by G.Harrison, Washington, 1951

The Struggle For Europe by Chester Wilmot. Collins, 1952

1944: The Canadians In Normandy by R.H.Roy. Macmillan, 1984

Dawn of D-Day by David Howarth. Fontana, 1961

The Longest Day by Cornelius Ryan. Simon and Schuster, 1959

D Day by Warren Tute and others. Sidgwick and Jackson, 1974

Decision in Normandy by C.D'Este. William Collins Sons, 1983.

Gauntlet to Overlord by R.Munro. MacMillan of Canada, 1945.

Six Armies in Normandy by J.Keagan. The Viking Press, 1982.

Overlord by M.Hastings. Guild Publishing, 1984.

My War by Andy A. Rooney. Adams Media Corporation, 1995.

The author, Dr. Reginald Roy was born in New Glasgow, Nova Scotia. During the Second World War he saw service in Canada, the Mediterranean and Northwest Europe. After the war Dr. Roy worked with Colonel C.P. Stacey and helped write the official history of the Canadian Army, 1939-45. From 1959 to the late 1980s he taught history at the University of Victoria. Now retired, Dr. Reginald Roy is the Honourary Lieutenant-Colonel of 741 (Victoria) Communication Squadron.